Printed in the United States of America

ISBN: 979-8-999-1178-0-9
Library of Congress Control Number: 2025911733
Cover and interior illustrations by Deniel Suarez
Shakira K. Williams. First edition.

For every curious child with a suitcase full of dreams and a heart ready to explore.

And to my dear son, Carter, may you always see the world with wonder and walk in it with courage and confidence.

— Shakira K. Williams

Namaste from India, a land so bright,
With dancing, spices, and colors of light.
See the Taj Mahal shining white and tall,
And join the kite festival—fun for all!

Olá from Brazil, where joy fills the air,
With dancers, music, and colors to spare.
Cristo Redentor stands open and wide,
Welcoming all with arms stretched with pride.

Bonjour from France, the land of art,
Where love and pastries fill every heart.
Climb the Eiffel Tower and take in the view,
And sail on the Seine with skies so blue.

Ciao from Italy, where pasta's king,
And gondolas glide as gondoliers sing.
Rome has ruins and stories so old,
And pizza ovens that never get cold!

Hello from Trinidad and Tobago, bright and bold,
With Carnival costumes trimmed in gold!
Hear steelpan rhythms fill the street,
And dance to the soca's lively beat.

Hola from Puerto Rico, vibrant and proud,
Where coquí frogs sing soft and loud.
Stroll through Old San Juan's colorful streets,
And taste sweet plantains—oh, what a treat!

Hey from Canada, big and grand,
With forests, lakes, and snowy land.
Climb the CN Tower so high in the sky,
And wave to the geese as they fly by!

Hello from England, with stories and charm,
Where Big Ben ticks and the Thames flows calm.
Ride the London Eye for views up high,
And watch red buses passing by!

Marhaba from the United Arab Emirates, land of gold,
Where stories of camels and towers unfold.
See the Burj Khalifa reach the skies,
And shop in souks with sparkling eyes.

Hola from Mexico, let's go explore,
To Chichén Itzá and ancient lore.
Walk around the stones so wide,
And hear the echoes from deep inside!

www.ingramcontent.com/pod-product-compliance
Lightning Source LLC
Chambersburg PA
CBHW080813120626

46556CB00009B/3311

* 9 7 9 8 9 9 9 1 1 7 8 2 3 *